# Pinhole Photographs

# Pinhole Photographs

Adam Fuss

Smithsonian Institution Press, Washington and London
Published in association with Constance Sullivan Editions

This series was developed and produced for the Smithsonian Institution Press
by Constance Sullivan Editions

Series editor:
Constance Sullivan

Smithsonian editor:
Amy Pastan

Designed by Katy Homans



Library of Congress Cataloging-in-Publication Data

Fuss, Adam.
Pinhole photographs : photographs / by Adam Fuss :
[edited by Constance Sullivan].
p. cm. — (Photographers at work)
"Published in association with Constance Sullivan Editions."
ISBN 1-56098-622-0 (paper)
1. Photography, Pinhole. 2. Fuss, Adam, 1961– .
I. Title. II. Series.
TR268.F87 1996
779'.092-dc20 95-3479
CIP

With thanks to Cajvan, Alessandra, Marco, Simone, Massimo, Agnes, and a kind woman in Paris.

The paper used in this publication meets the minimum requirements of the
American National Standard for Permanence of Paper for Printed Library Materials
Z39.48-1984.



First edition

Printed by The Stinehour Press, Lunenburg, Vermont

**Describe the origins of your involvement with photography.**

When I was about fifteen I became interested in photography through a friend who knew all about lenses and cameras and equipment. I obsessed about the Olympus OM I and how I needed that "great" camera to work with. I didn't get one for a few years. I was given a less sophisticated camera by my mother. I just liked gadgetry. When I started taking pictures I showed them to my art teacher. I apologized to him that my camera wasn't very good and he said, "Well, it doesn't matter. You can take the best pictures in the world with a pinhole camera."

**What kind of pictures were you taking?**

My first project was photographing a barn owl flying in and out of a hollow tree.

**I can see the relationship of that to your later work.**

I can, too. Then, after school, I went to Australia to get a job in a photo studio. I took classes from a professional photographer named Graham McCarter who showed us famous photographs. That's really where I saw photographs for the first time.

**You didn't grow up with any of the divisions—street vs. studio—that have plagued students of American photography?**

I grew up in complete ignorance, photographically speaking.

**How did you support yourself in Australia?**

I worked in the darkroom of the photography studio for Ogilvy & Mather, printing and processing stuff. I started experimenting with color film. I felt I wasn't very good compared to the other people. We had a lecture by a man named John Williams who took pictures of people moving in the street with a flash. That was inspiring to me. I started experimenting with that technique when I came to New York. But I didn't do it in the street. I lived in Williamsburg, in Brooklyn, which at the time was filled with empty buildings. I would go around and photograph objects that people had left behind. I mixed daylight and flash, using multiple exposures, turning the camera upside down and other crazy stuff. I made a series of pictures called "Details in Deserted Buildings," and I showed them as slide shows for friends. I did one show at the Pyramid Club. But otherwise almost no one saw the work.

**When and why did you start the pinhole series?**

When I first arrived in New York, I worked at the Metropolitan Museum. Sometimes I'd be walking at night through the classical sculpture galleries. The figures have a certain kind of life, perhaps because their life span is so much longer than ours. They've seen generations of people walk past. In the daytime the museum environment seemed so *inappropriate.* But at night they'd come alive, full of power and mystery. When I thought about taking these pinhole pictures I thought of my experience of walking through these galleries at night, completely alone, and that teacher's words, about the pinhole camera, came back to me. It seemed possible to create or recreate a photographic space in which the sculptures could "breathe." Also behind my move in this direction was a reaction to the pervasive technological-consumerist photographic culture.

**You worked on the series for how long?**

I worked hard for two years. I didn't work in any other way. I made two trips to Europe to photograph sculpture. But I didn't have any money. It was the kindness of friends and strangers that made this work possible. In the end someone offered me an exhibition.

**Did your work with photograms evolve from the pinhole material?**

Yes. I was in Washington, photographing the White House and I spaced out and forgot to uncover the pinhole. When I processed that sheet of film later I noticed that the cardboard box wasn't sealed. Light had leaked in and made a photogram of the dust on the inside of the camera. I realized this was a way to make a picture without the outside world. I could generate pictures myself.

**How did you survive in those years?**

I supported myself as a commercial photographer for art galleries in the East Village, taking pictures of paintings and sculpture and installations.

**You began to make photograms in '86 and '87. Did you gradually wean yourself away or was it a drastic change of procedure?**

It was pretty sudden. I did a bunch of experiments by putting things in the enlarger and projecting them on paper. Twisted cellophane. Soap bubbles. But the first time I felt strongly about these experiments was when I worked with the motion of water. I woke up one morning with an image in mind. There is one particular photograph that led me in this direction. I had been doing these experiments with color film and the pinhole. They were circular images, multiple pinholes, dots of light. I had some film in the refrigerator that had gotten wet and moldy. I processed it and it produced this very beautiful color thing. I loved it. It was like a jewel. That was another transitional picture from the pinhole to the photogram.

**How do you feel about your photograms of water?**

They're still among my favorites. I made large images of the wave from a single drop of water, and of snakes swimming through water and moving about on powdered surfaces. I made a series by mounting a light on a pendulum. That switched into color, and then I made the photograms of babies.

**Do the children and the babies have particular metaphoric significance or autobiographic import?**

My pictures are always metaphorical. At that time in my life I felt that I came in contact with information that gave me the possibility of a spiritual life. Those pictures are a direct reference to that, to something within my body (like a child). I don't want to elaborate too much.

**When did you make the photograms of the babies and the "Details of Love" series?**

The babies are from about '92, after the dark children. "Details of Love" came out of the picture called "Love": two rabbits with their guts intertwined. I wanted to make a picture that was both abstract and figurative at the same time. Those two modes of representation were to have an intimate connection. I took a fish and took the guts out, leaving it connected at the anus and the mouth. With the intestine you have this certain quality of line—a cliché of abstraction. In '91, an emotionally "gut-wrenching" time, the idea of going back to this work came to me. I wanted to work with a horse. But the rabbit turned out to be perfect as it's so symbolically absorbent. I made a lot of pictures. It was hard to do. The colors in the pictures come from the bonding of the chemistry in the intestines and the chemistry of the paper.

**The rabbit pictures seem loaded with meaning, about death and the evisceration of life.**

Yes, I think of them as being about life and living. They are also about the internal entanglement with another person, sexual, generative forces, loss, and the act of sacrifice.

**And now you're working with stained-glass windows, which combine the Iconography of Christianity with the transforming power of light. How did you start on this series?**

Being translucent, stained glass is a material with characteristics that predispose me toward it. I used to visit this abandoned church in London and see kids throw rocks through the windows. I thought I would like to collect those fragments and, through my work, bring them back, make them whole, using those kids' energy as a catalyst. I began to experiment and I came up with this process where I could leave the silver in the paper. The first time I saw it I thought, "This is like seeing stained glass by moonlight." It was an experience I realized that I had never had. Then I realized a Christian church is really a form of solar temple. I felt that I had found the appropriate light for these things being broken and removed from their original structure. There seems to be a correspondence between lunar and silver symbolism and the photography and its chemistry. That was something I was interested in before. But here it became directly manifest.

**How do you know when you've found a pregnant image, something you want to make into a series?**

I have an idea and then explore it. My ideas are already encoded with the requisite data about how it will work photographically. I make images in my head the same way I make them on paper. It's only when I make a picture that I have to keep looking at that I feel I've succeeded. I've always needed to make images that have a sense of revelation to the viewer, namely me.

**When you look at it you're surprised at yourself?**

No, not at myself. It's more like the sensation of looking into the face of someone very beautiful. Or, perhaps, when our ancestors were in the village and the first time they saw a car or an airplane, where the image is so captivating, so fresh, so new that it takes you out of your normality for a little while. You're faced with the unknown. I got into pinhole and photograms because I was bored with the pictures I was seeing.

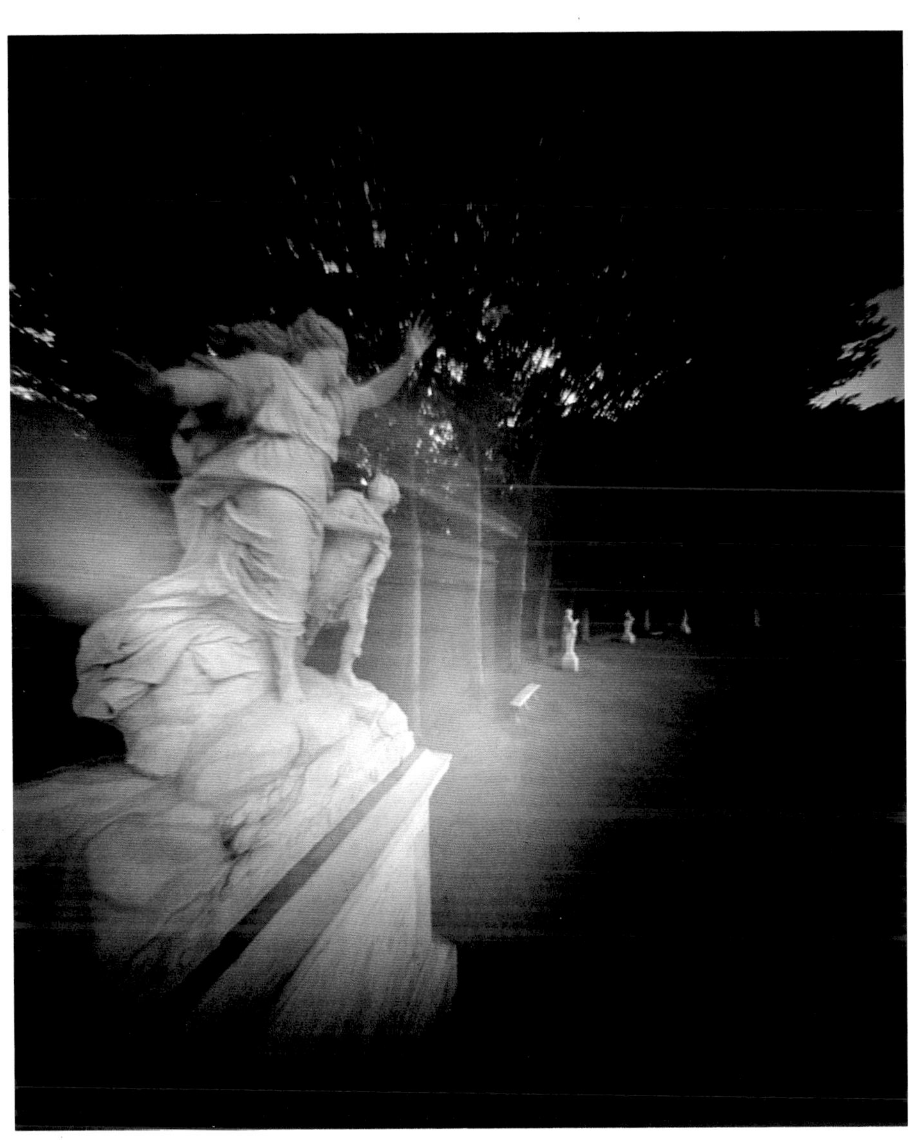

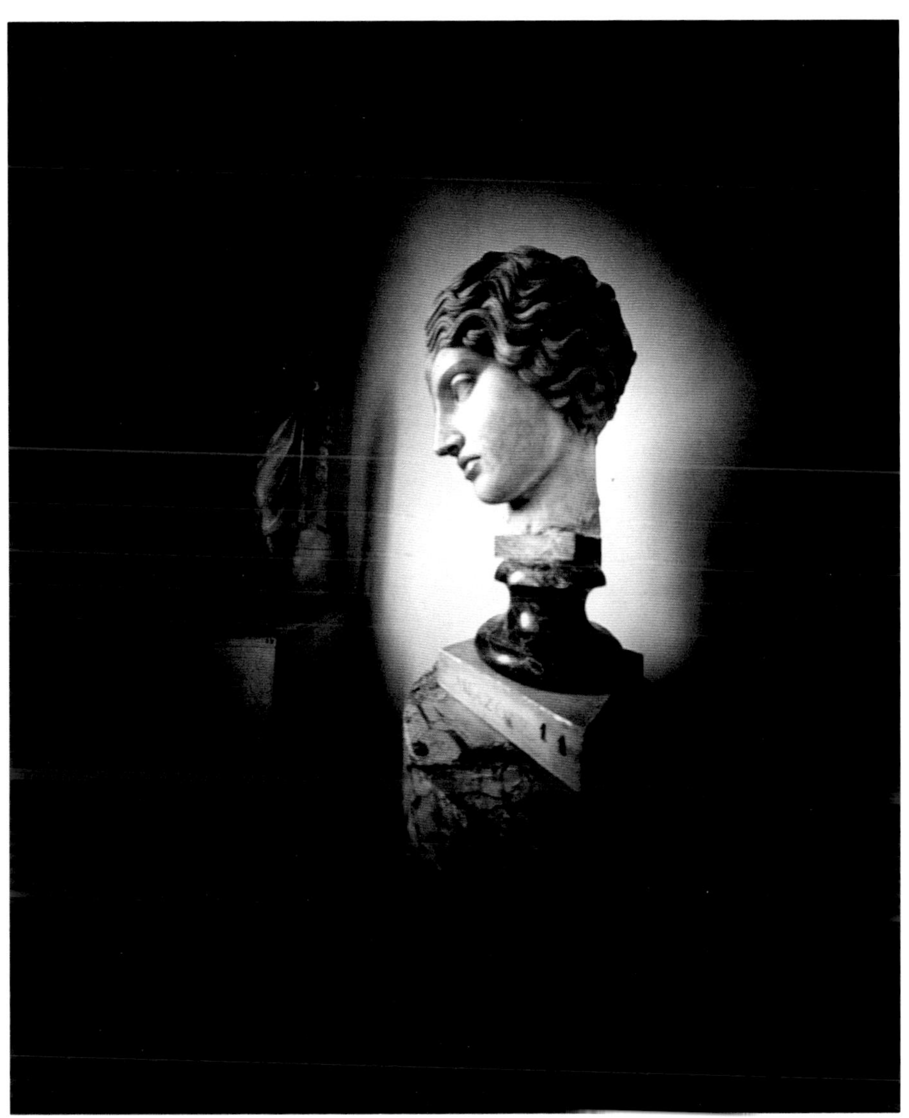

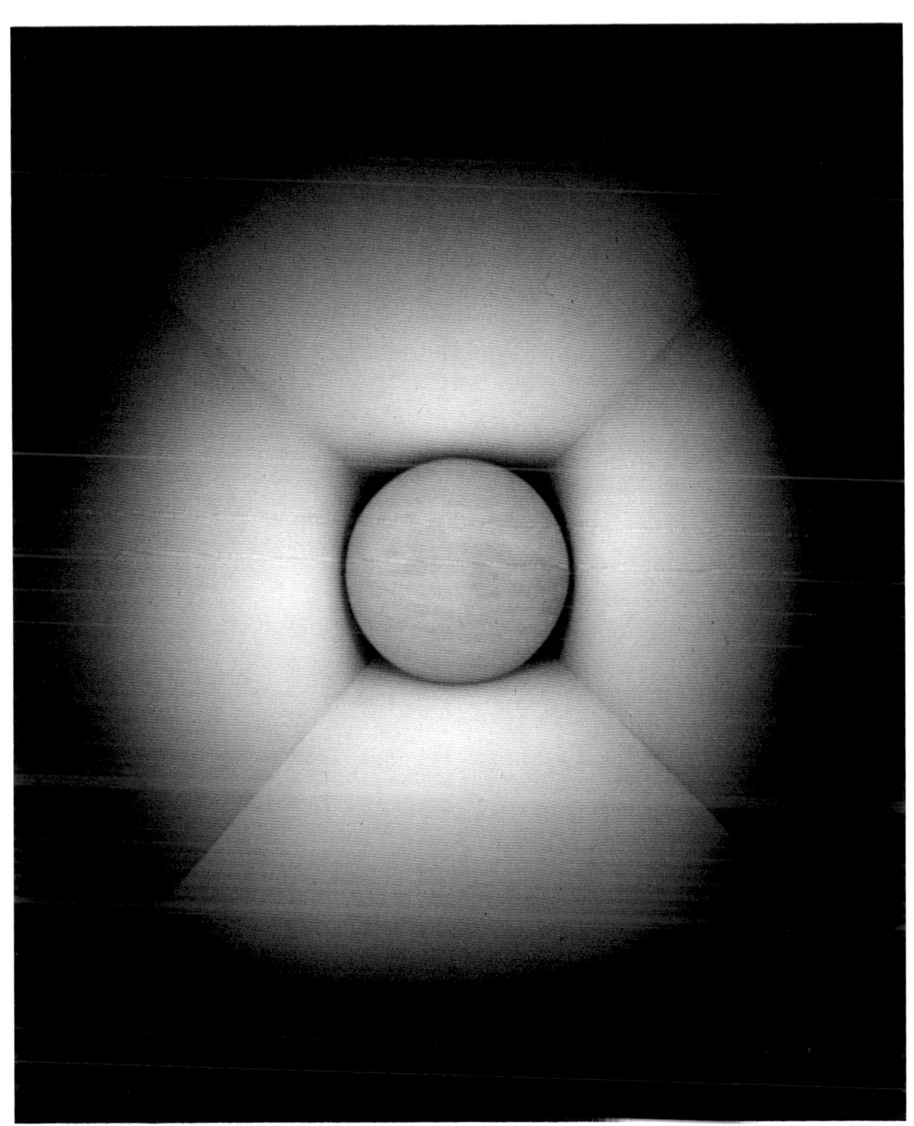

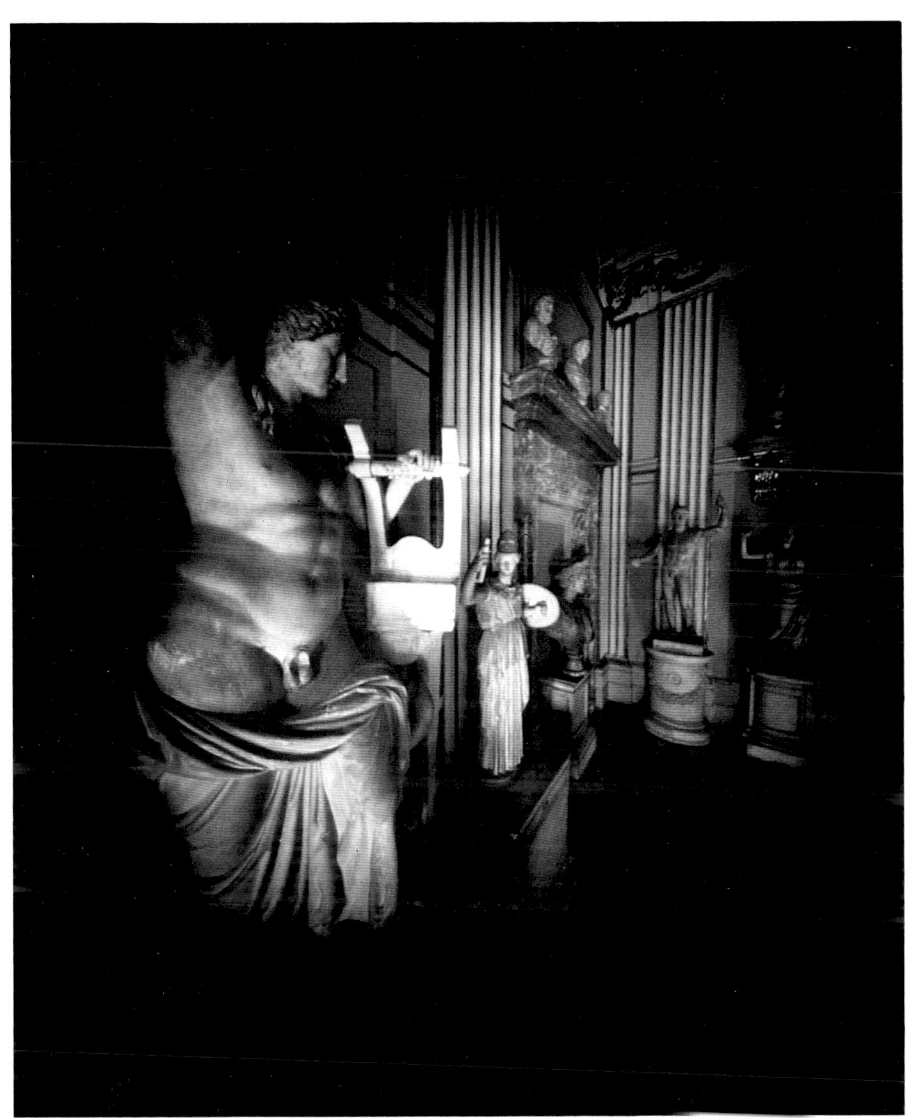

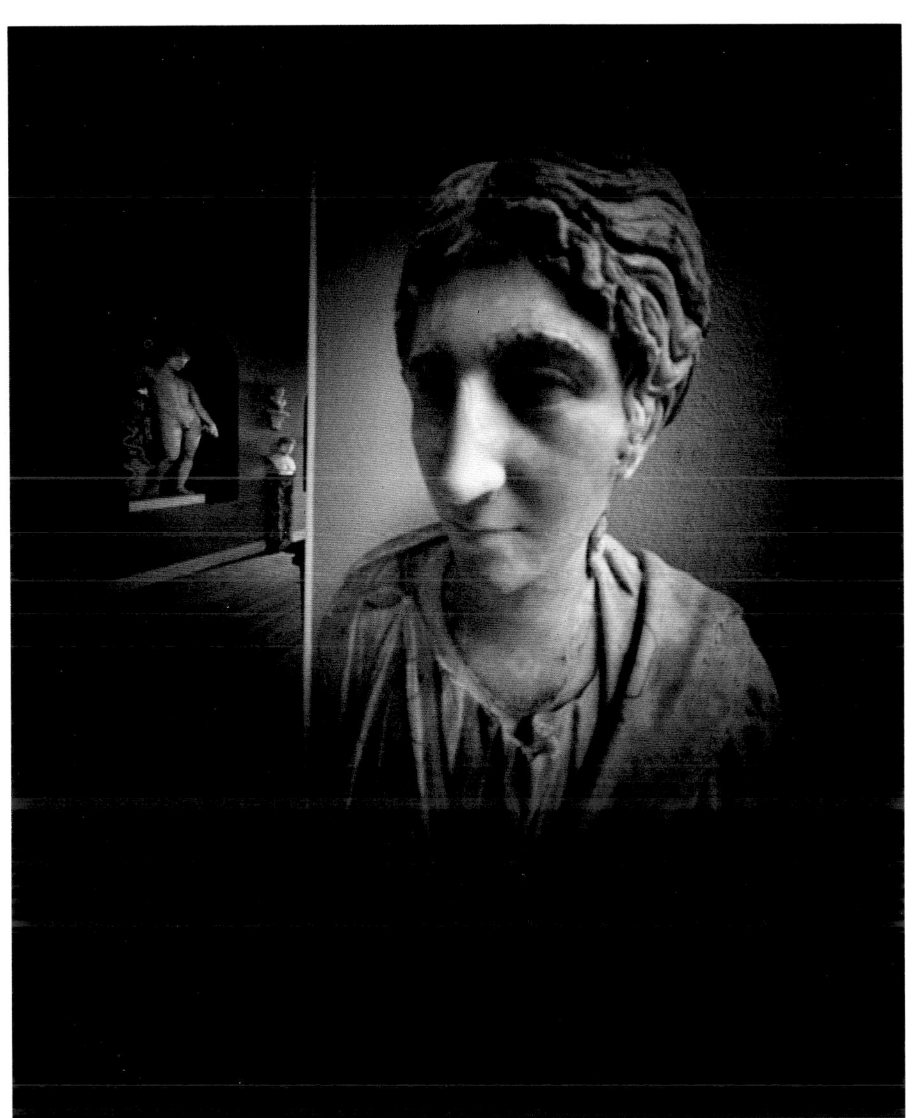

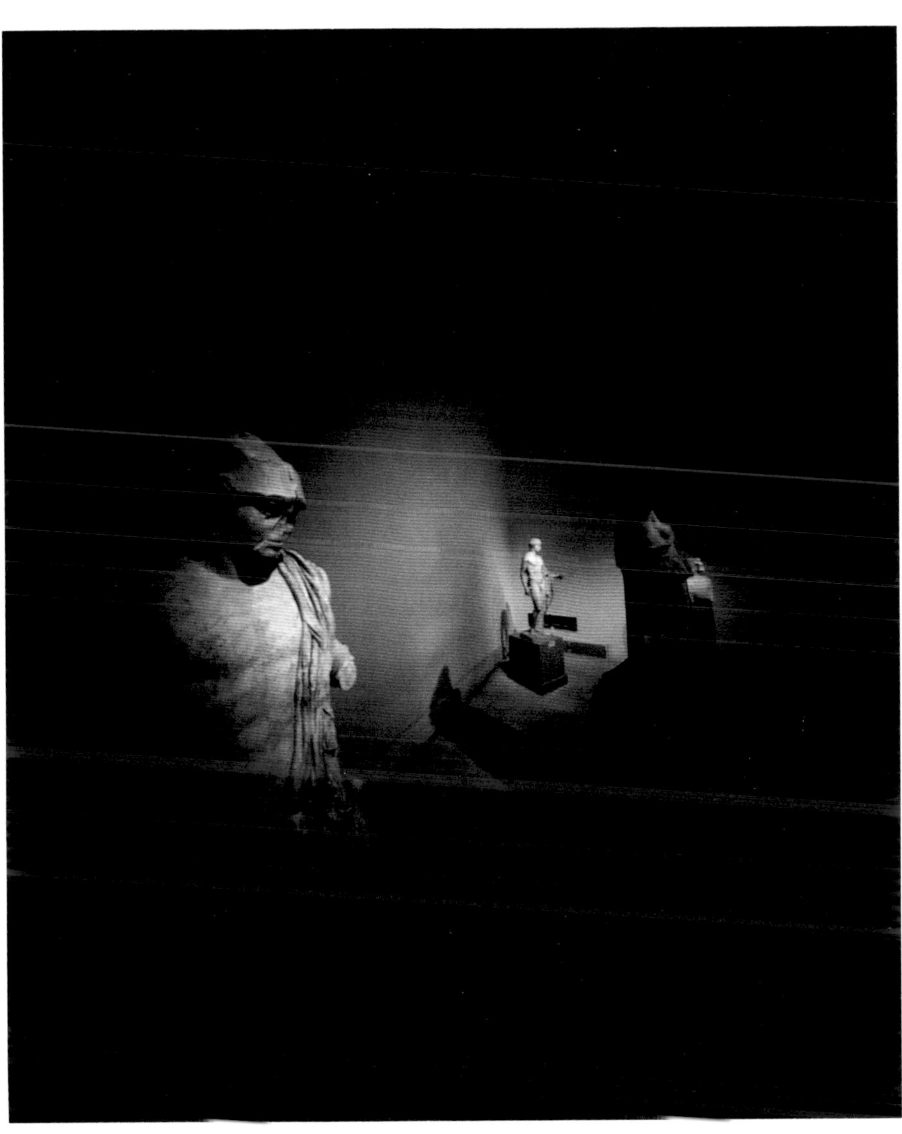

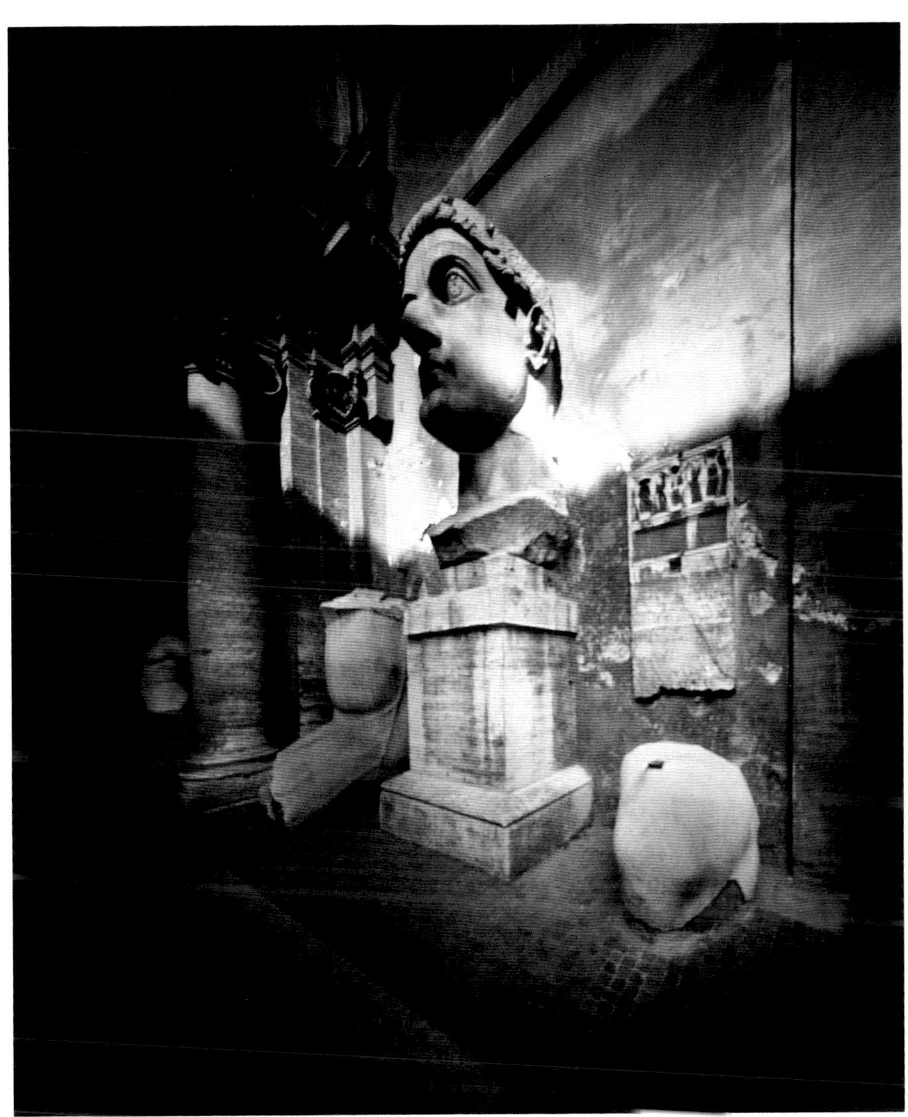

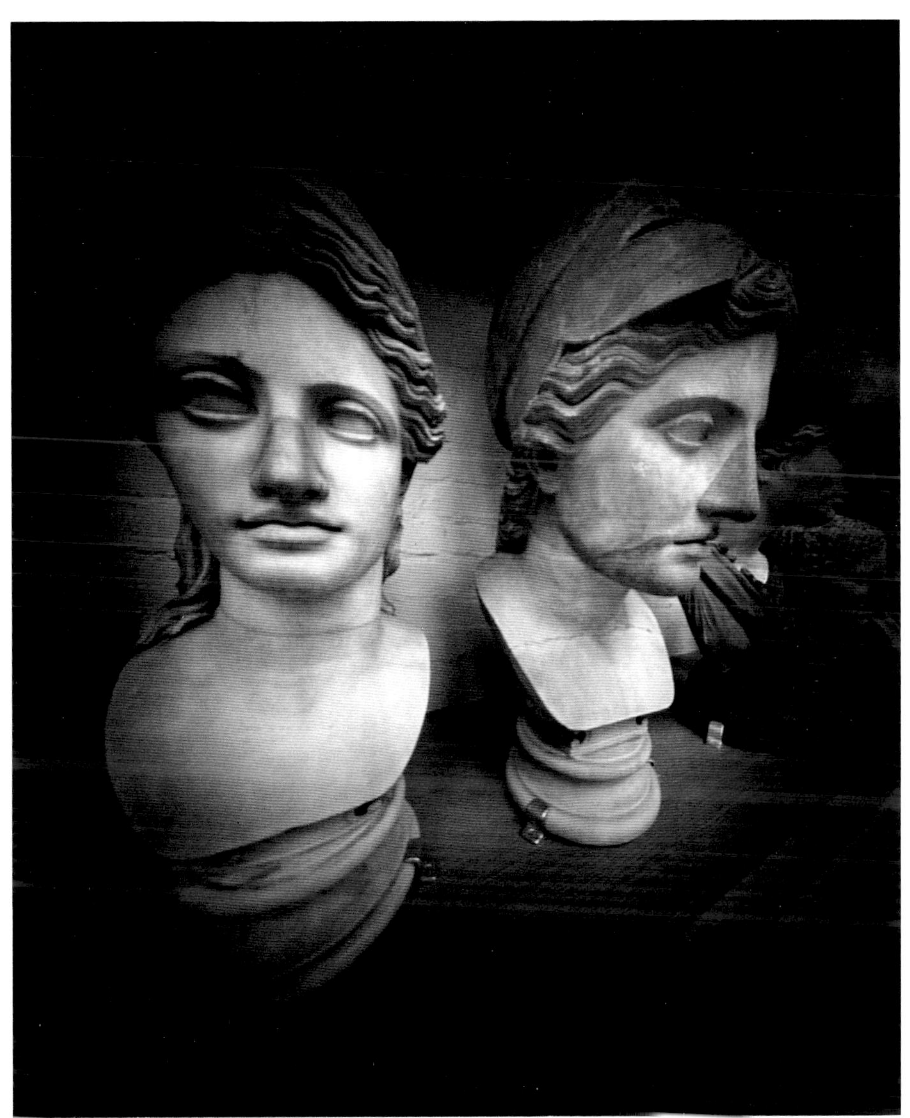

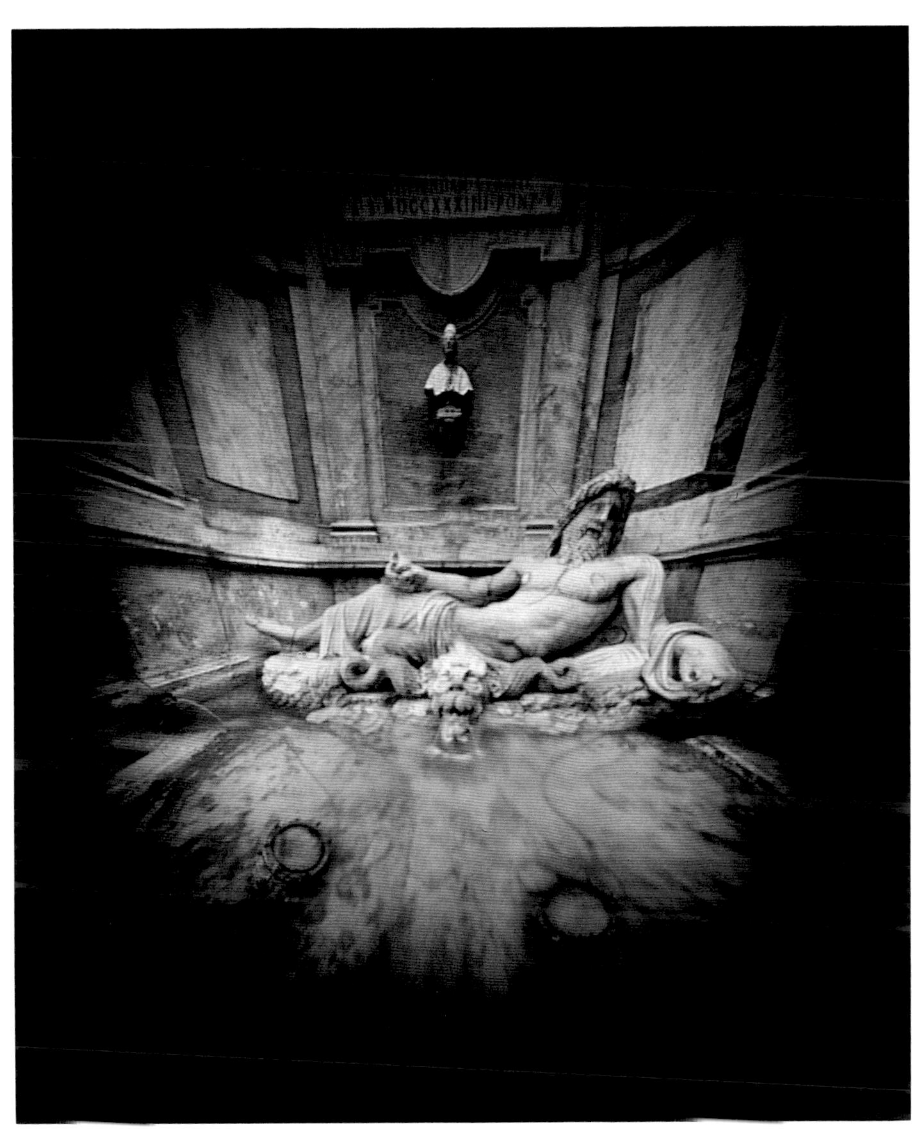

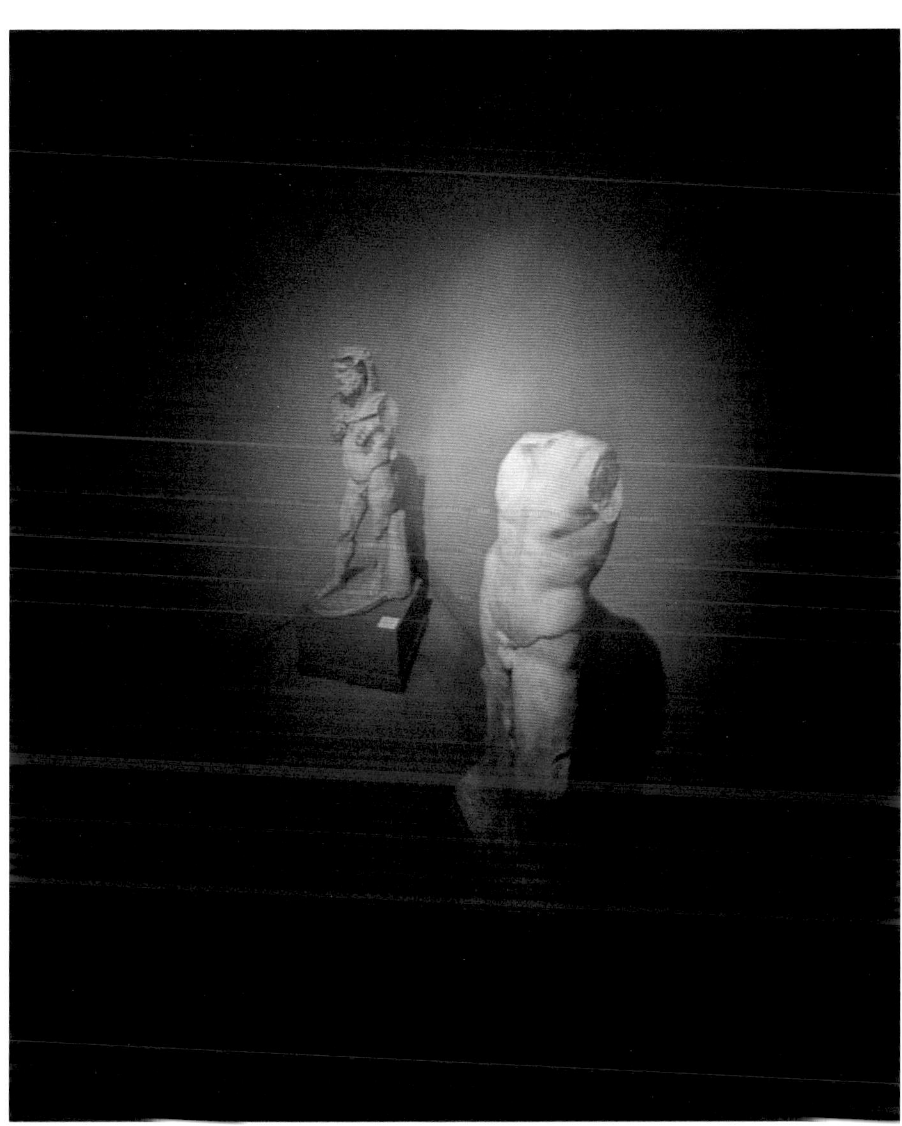

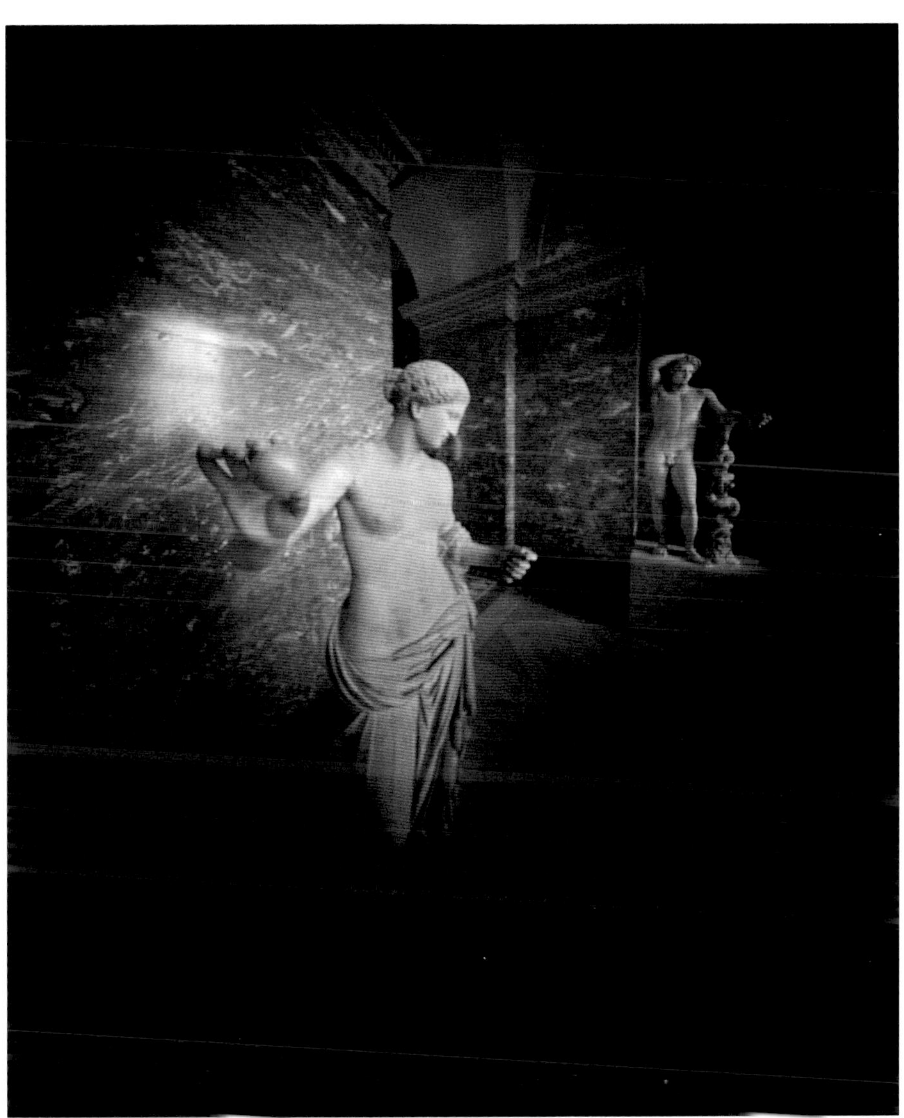

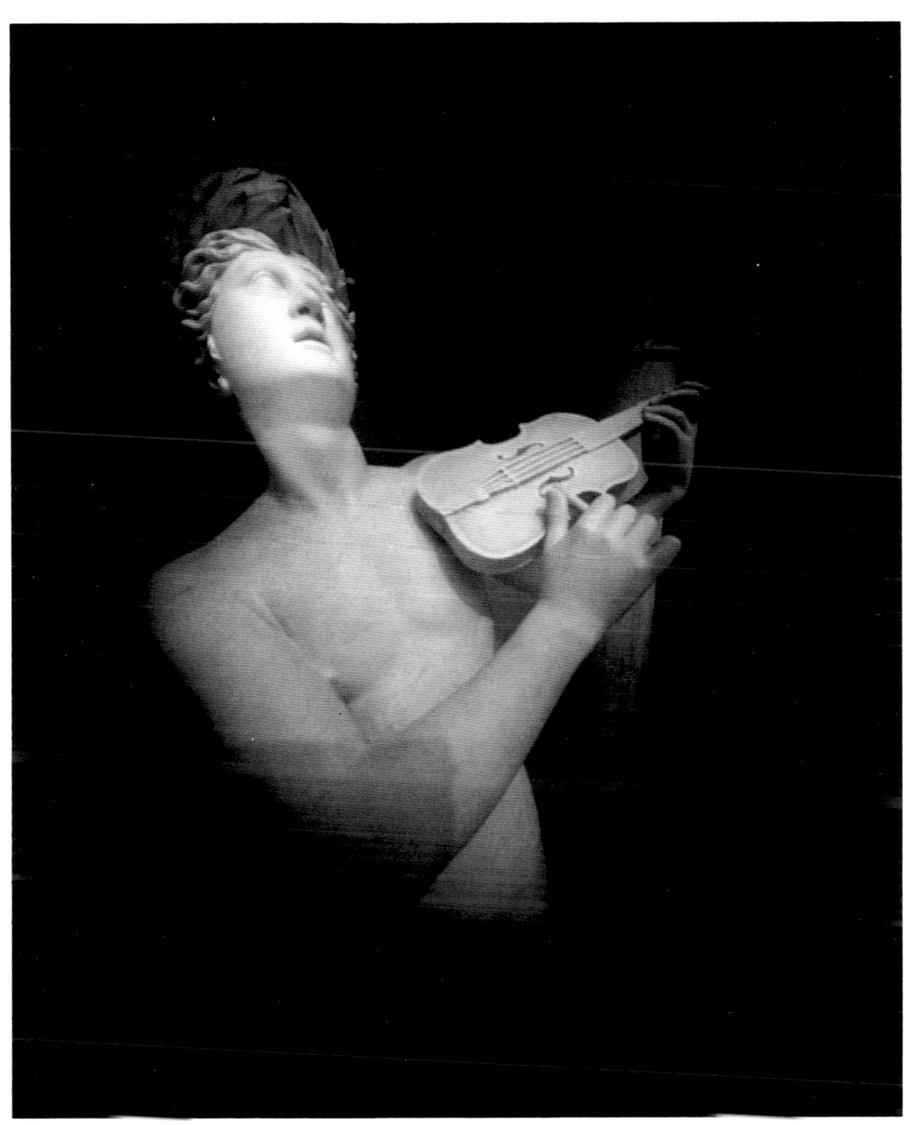

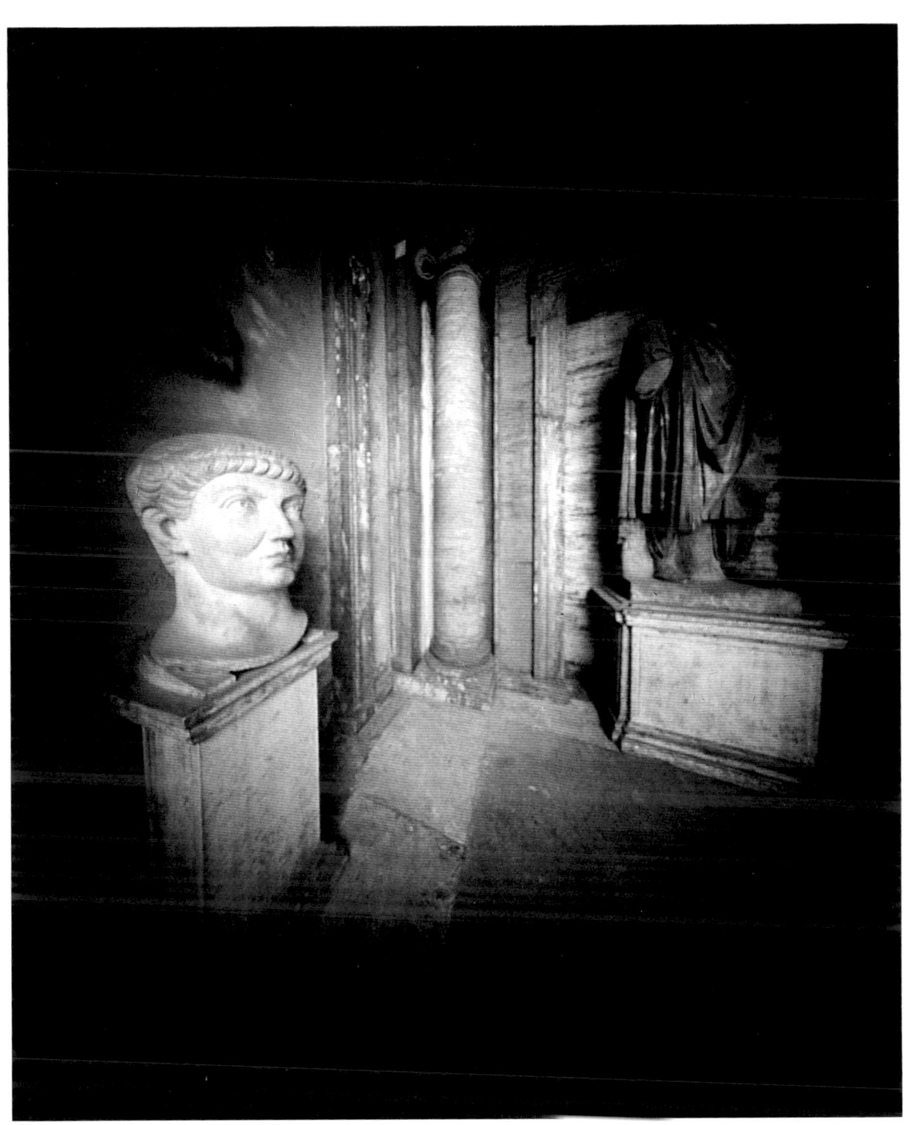

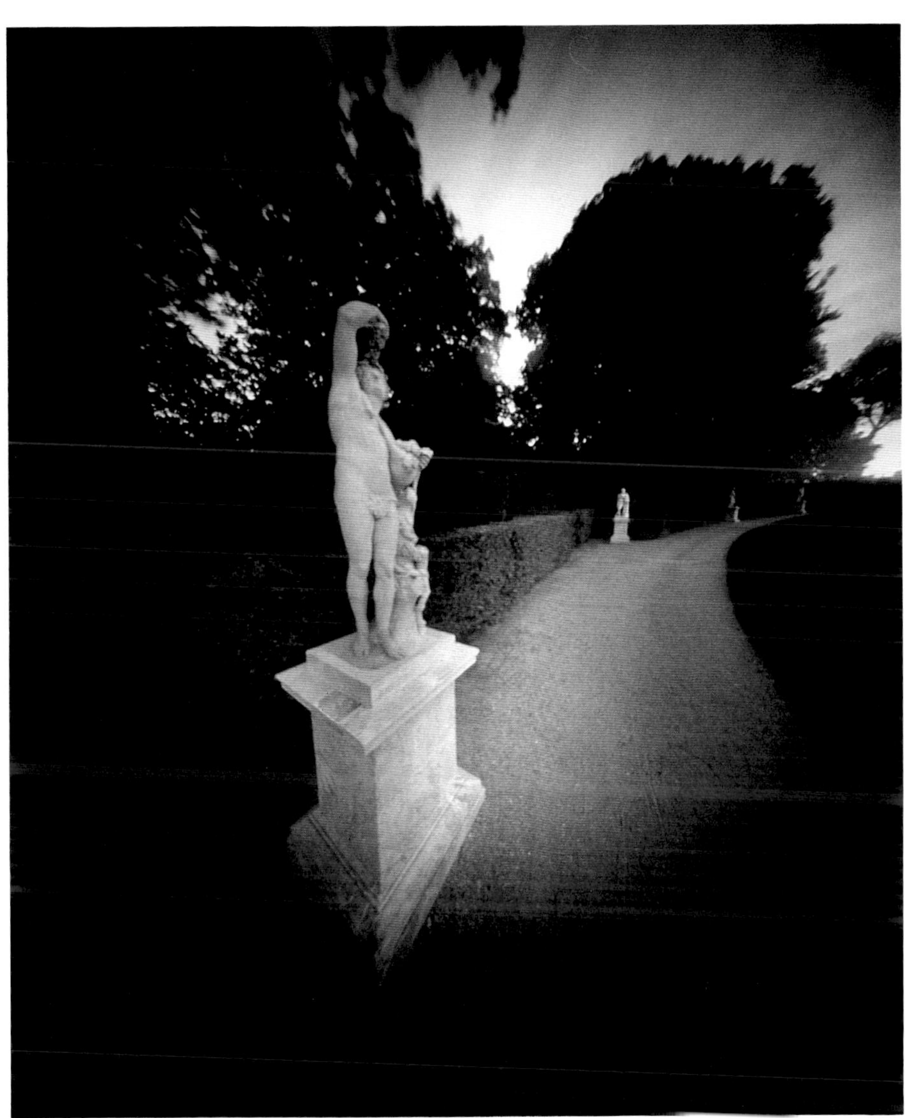

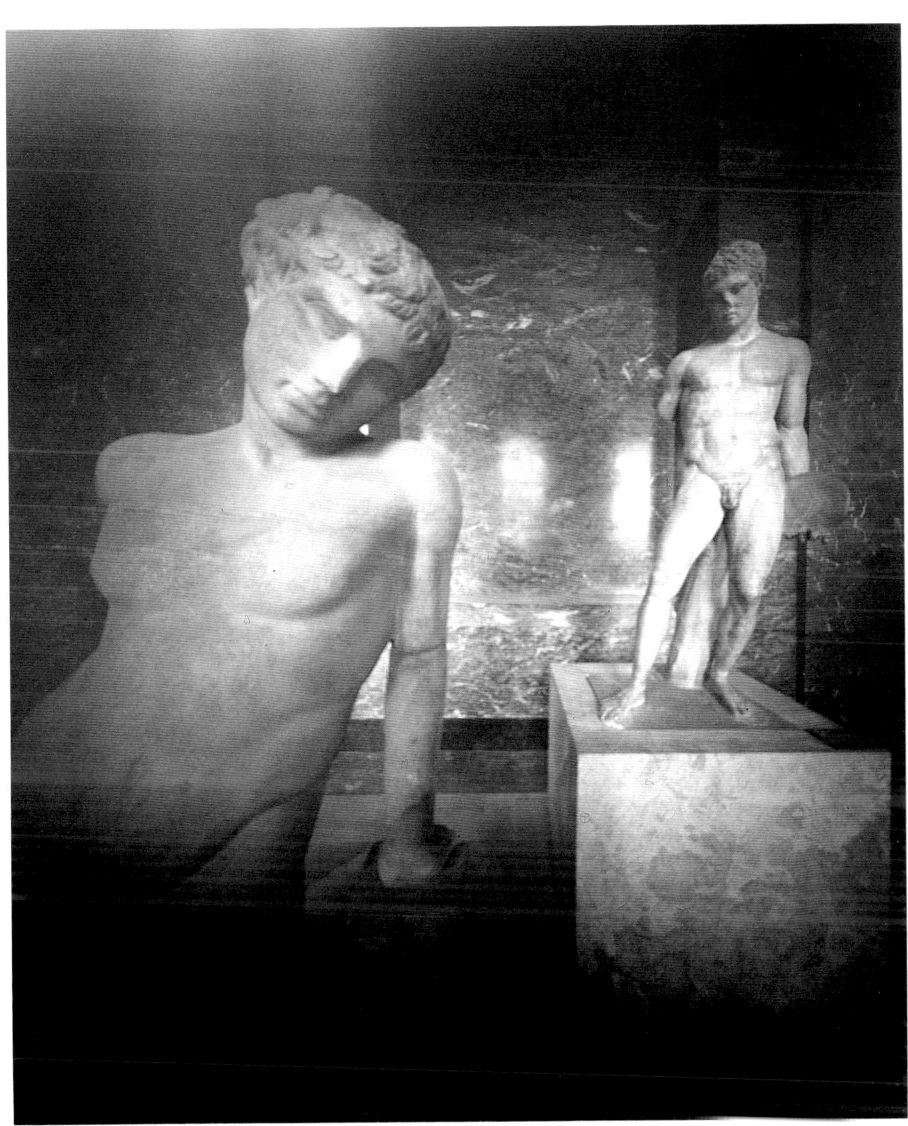

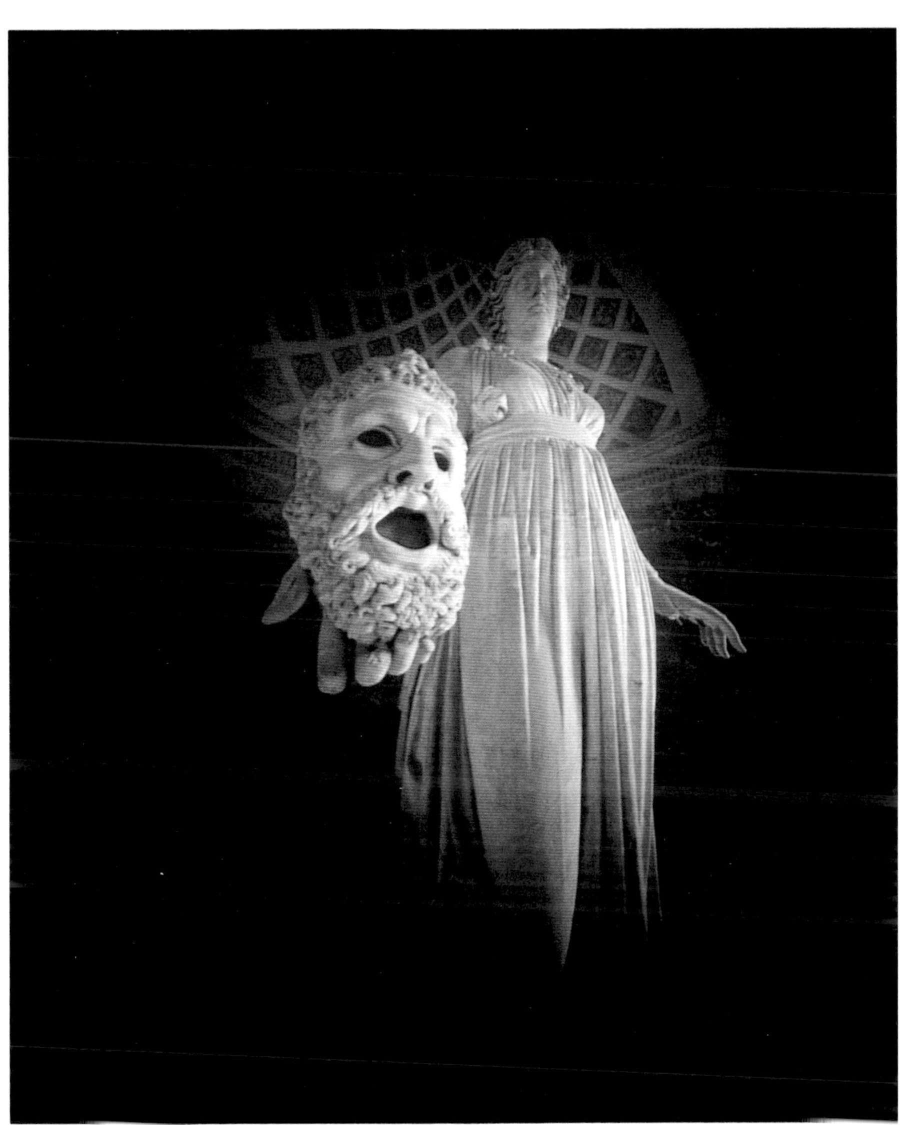

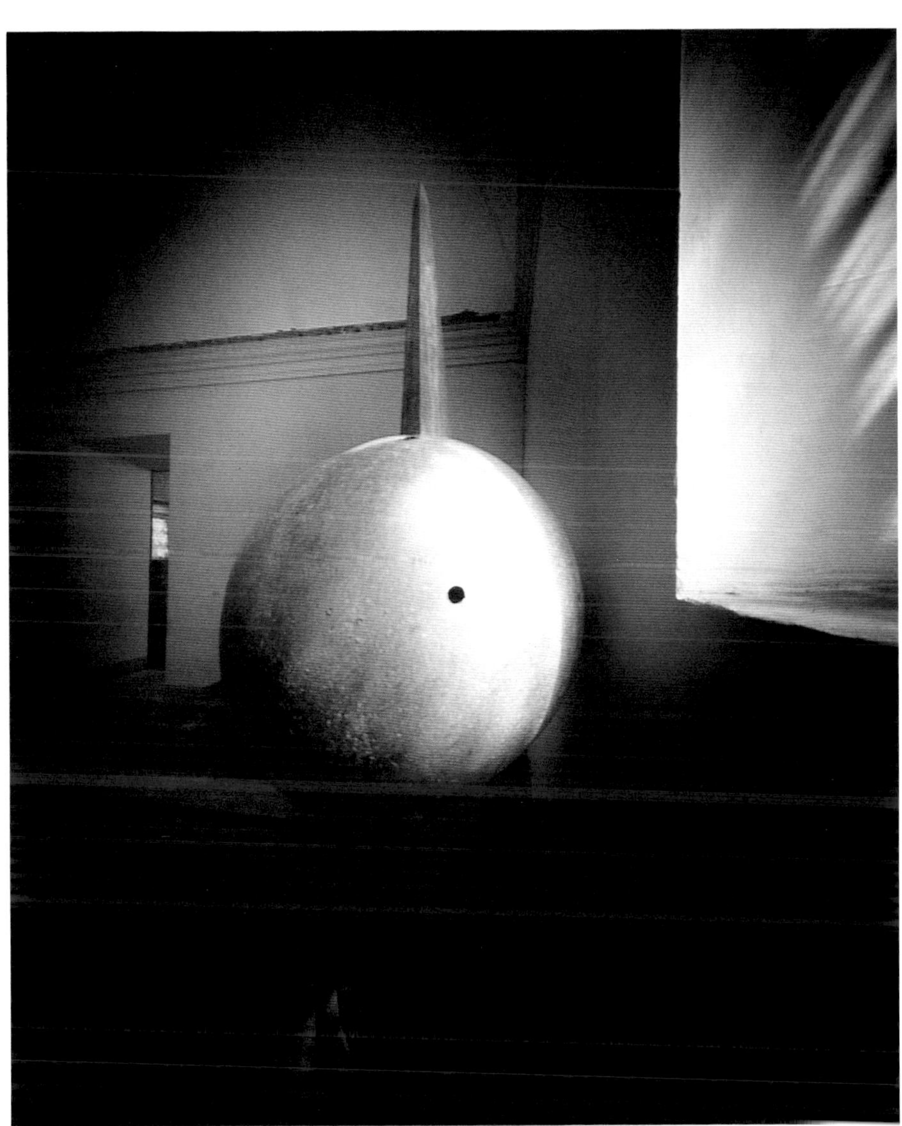

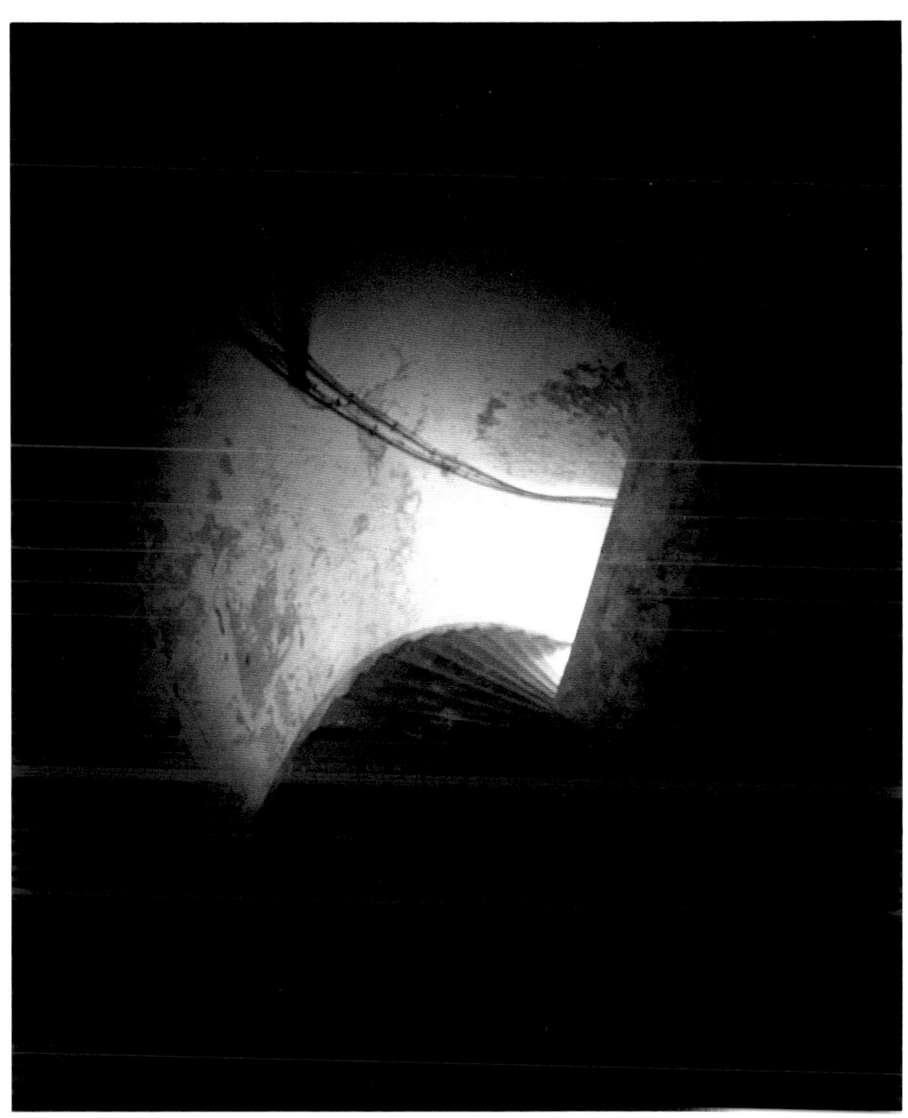

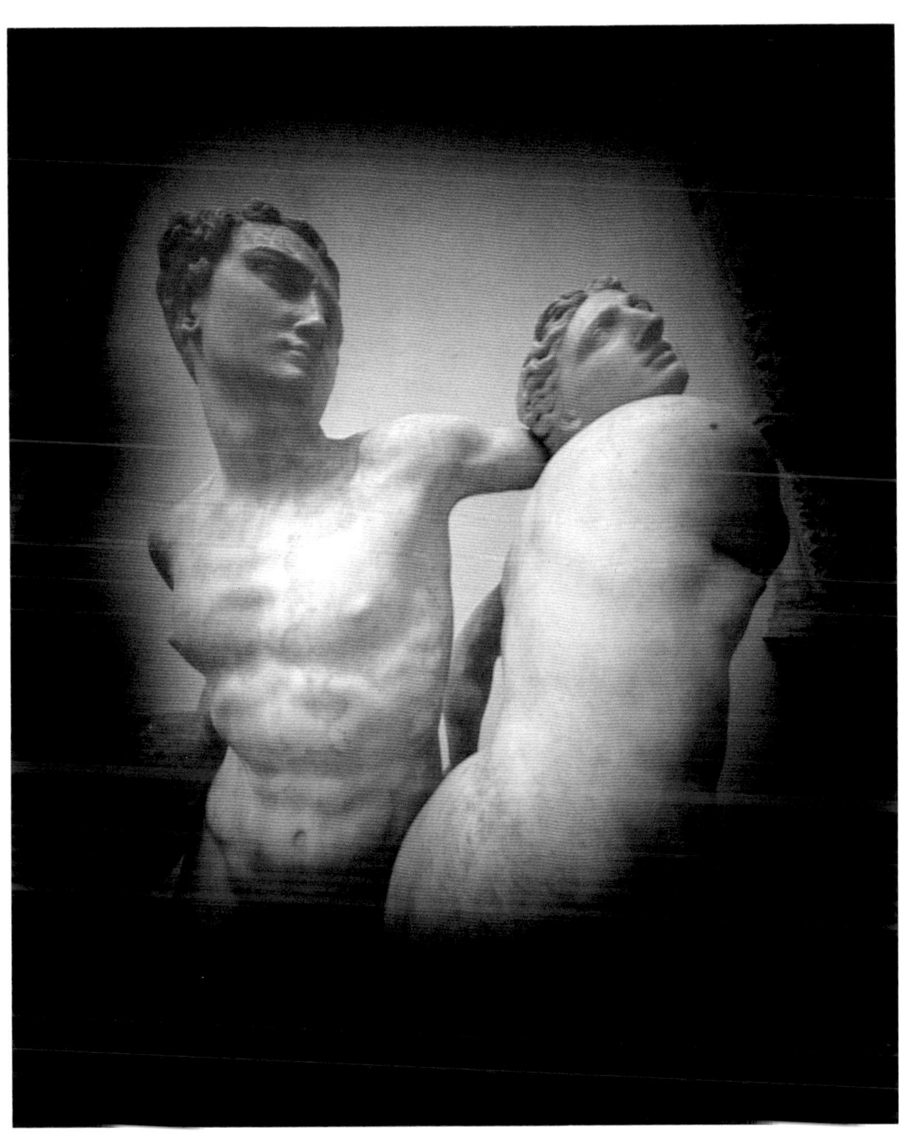

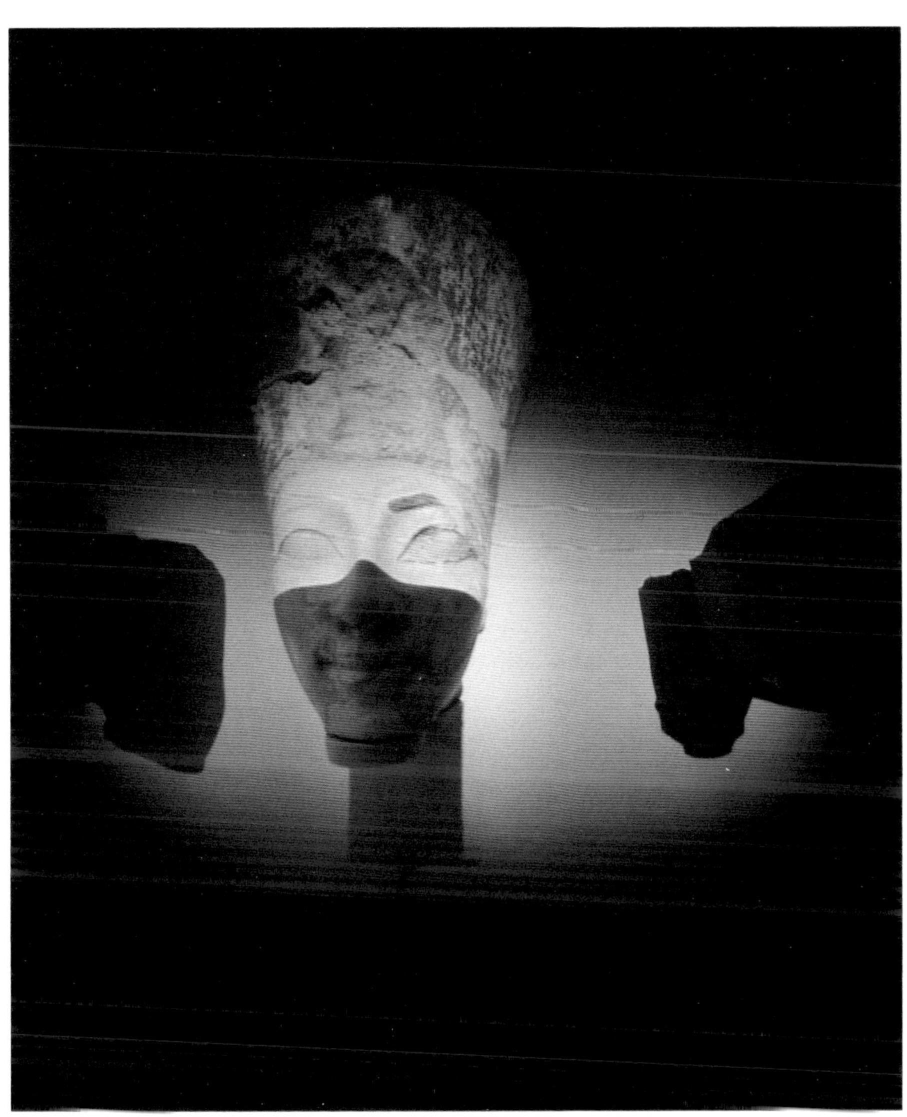

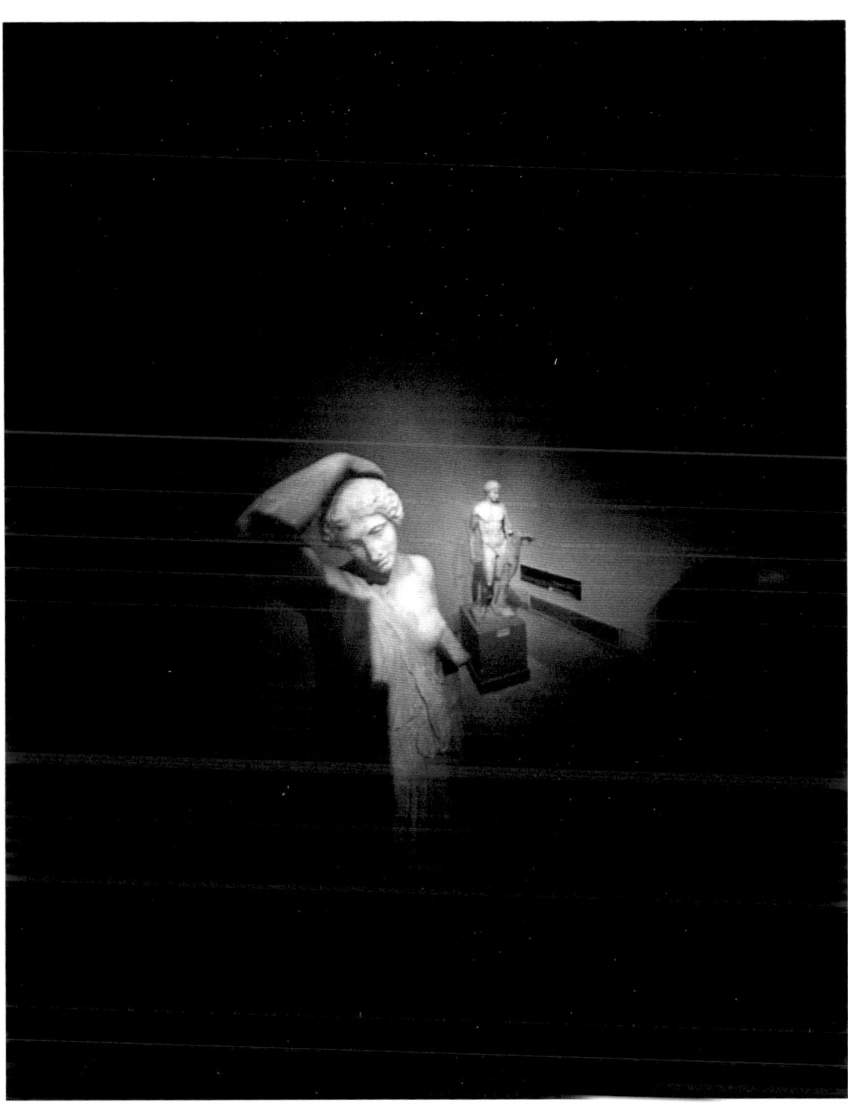

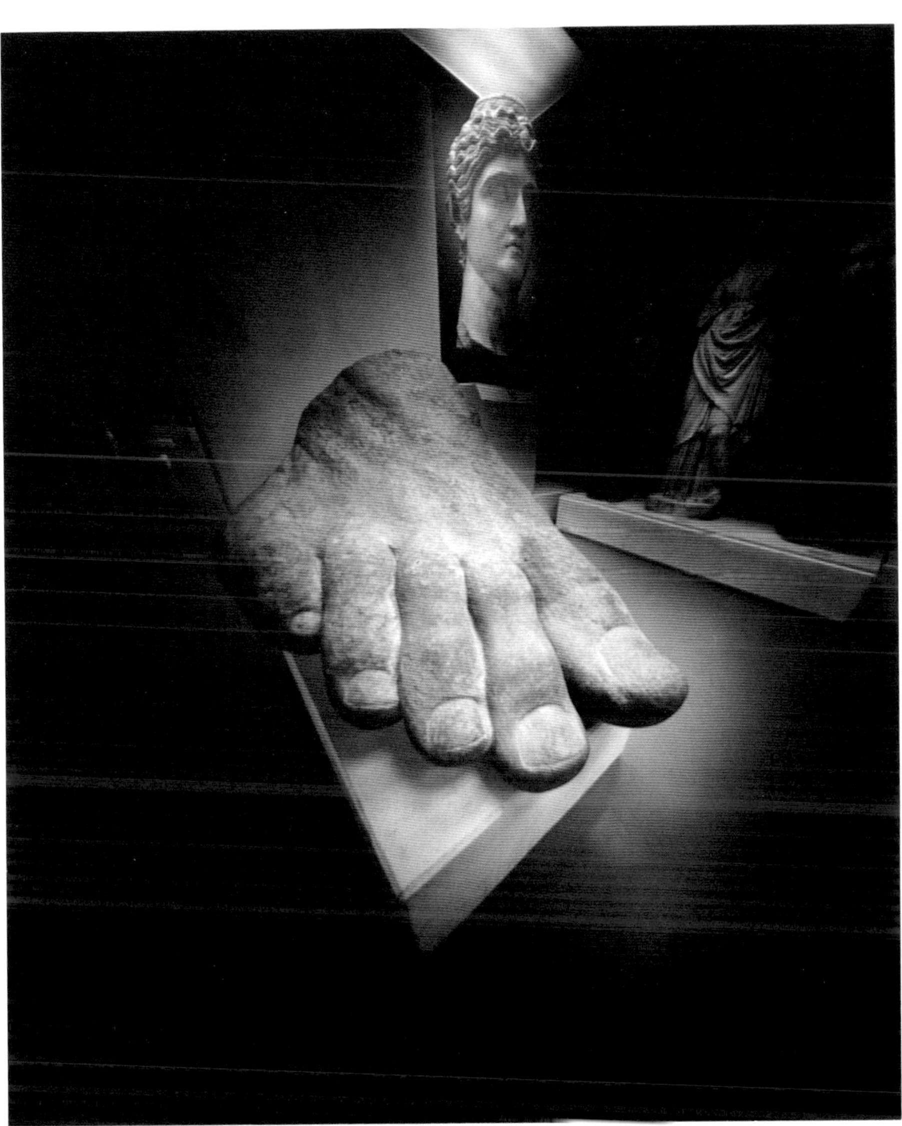

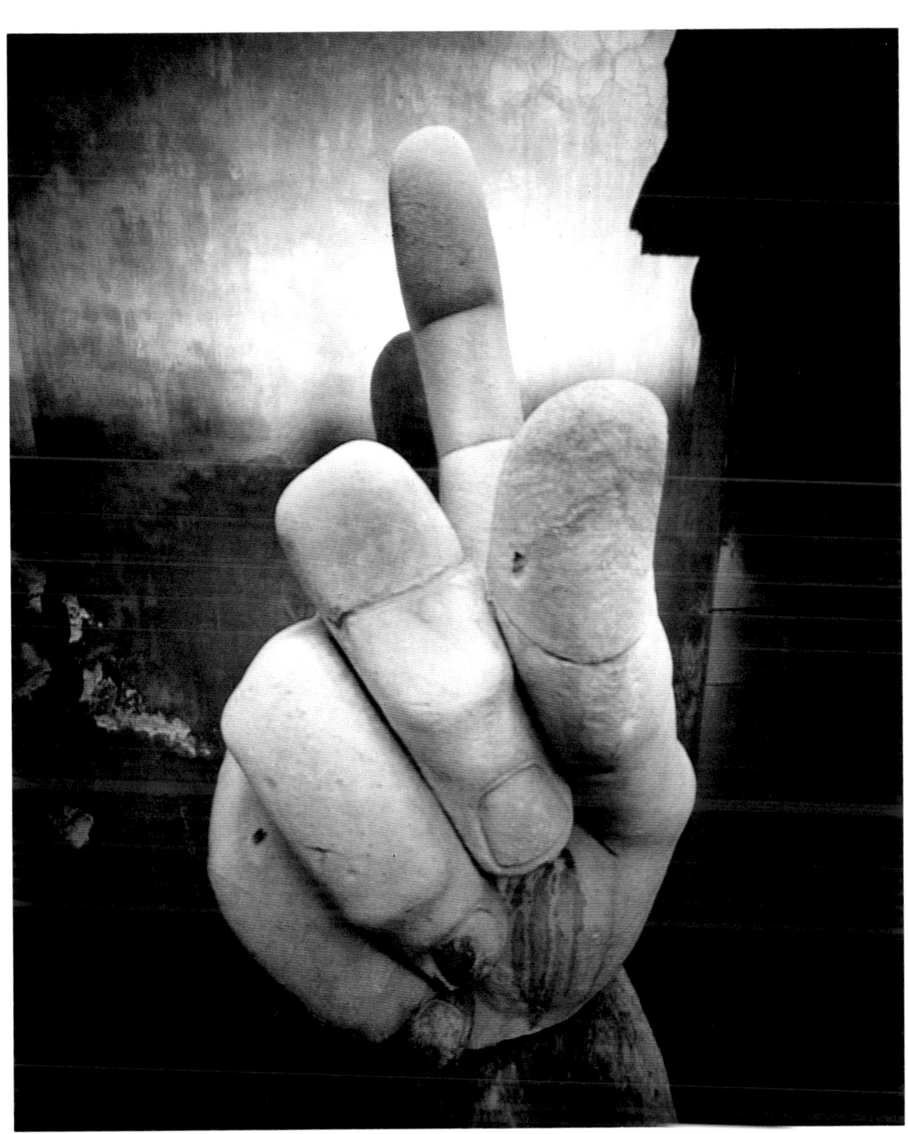

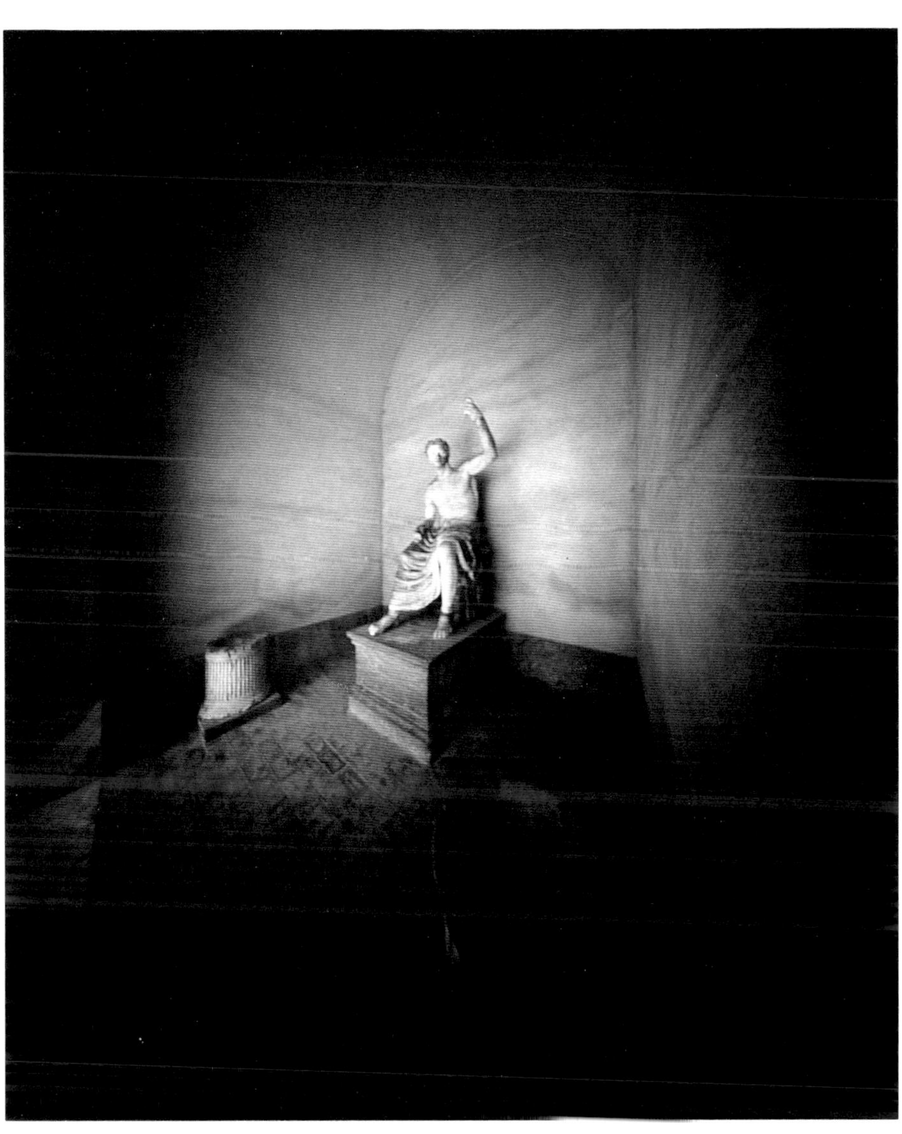

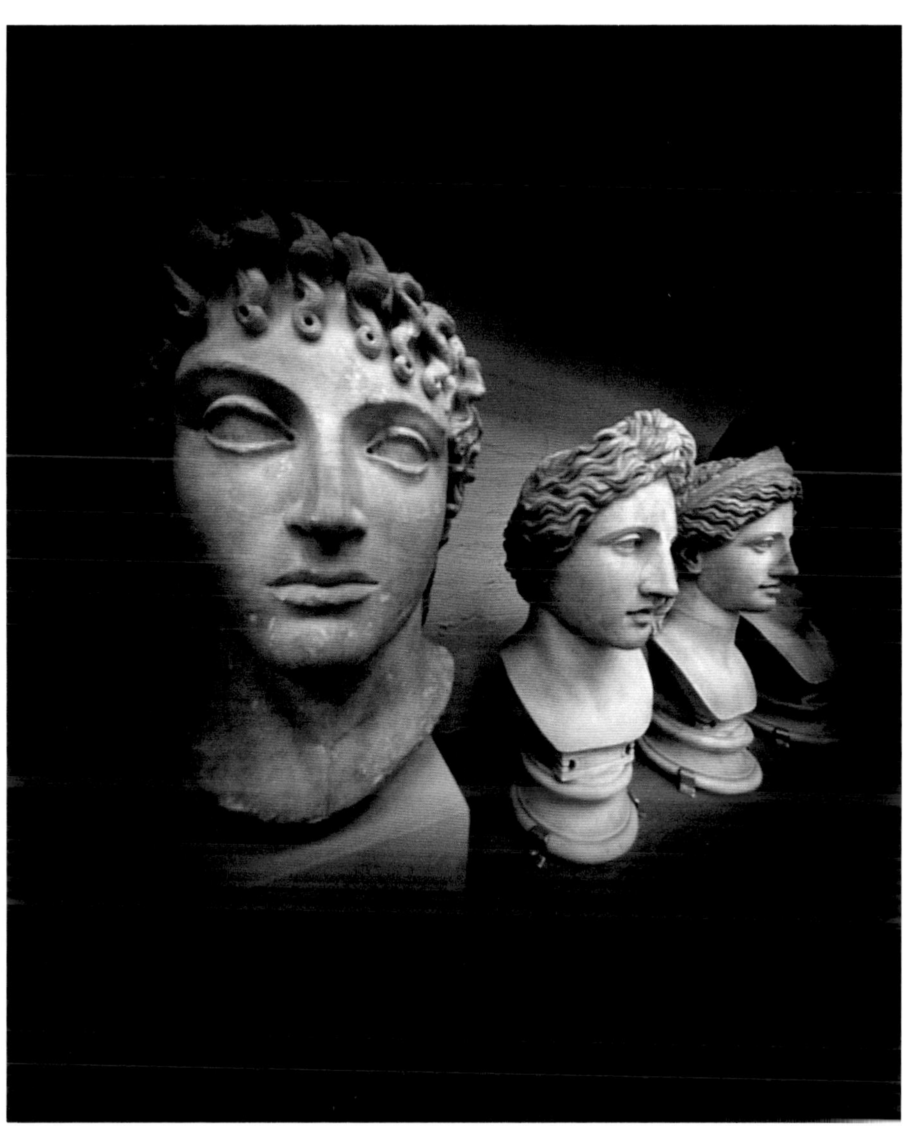

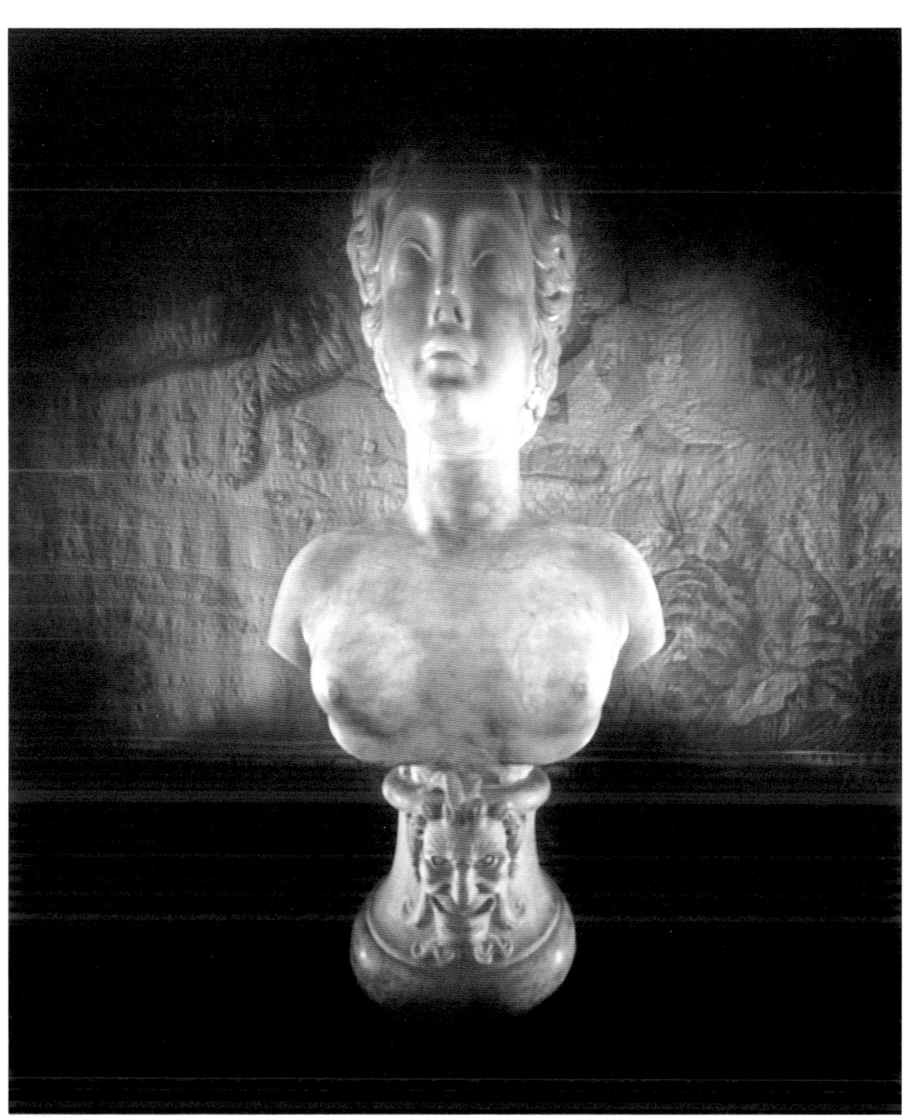

# Adam Fuss

Adam Fuss makes incandescent images with some of the most ordinary tools at the disposal of a photographer. Whether he is warping single-point perspective with a handmade pinhole camera or abjuring cameras altogether in his photograms, he relies on the basic principles of photo-chemistry to conjure up a primal reality. His pictures can seem like records of an earlier time when dreaming and seeing were not yet separate activities of the mind. One of the major artists of his generation, he has been a leader in showing how much photographers have to gain by returning the medium to its origins as a kind of industrial-age alchemy.

Born in London and raised in rural England, he came to photography as a teenager. His interest at that age was primarily technological. He learned to develop and print his own pictures, and he embarked on several long-term projects that allowed him to experiment with equipment and venture into the countryside. After grammar school, he set off for Australia to work as an assistant in a photo studio where he encountered a teacher who exposed him for the first time to art photography. Fuss remembers being especially impressed by the ominous images of Bill Brandt and Eugene Meatyard, even though he experienced them mainly through reproductions on slides.

At the age of 21, he moved to New York. In the Williamsburg section of Brooklyn, where he first lived, he photographed the insides of abandoned buildings, mixing flash with natural light to capture the spookiness of dereliction. This series of pictures eventually became a slide show that he presented to groups of friends in informal settings.

His experiments with the pinhole camera grew out of a desire to create three-dimensional images that could hang on a wall. Fuss became a fringe member of the young and burgeoning art scene on the Lower East Side of Manhattan, supporting himself as a photographer for the many galleries then springing up. He had his first one-person show—the pinhole pictures of sculpture in the museums of New York, Washington, and Europe—at Massimo Audiello Gallery in 1985.

Since the mid-'80s Fuss has devoted most of his imaginative energy to the photogram. A prolific and restless artist, he has tinkered with various light sources, printing papers, and translucent objects. He sees the last fifteen years of his development as a photographic tool-user—from the high-tech SLR to the aleatoric, low-budget atmospherics of the pinhole to the cameraless photogram—as a process of increasing internalization.

As he has reached inside the camera and pulled his images out of the film itself, or built them up out of objects placed within the enlarger or on the surface of photographic paper, he has become less dependent on the ocular world. The materials for his work have reflected this surgical invasion, especially his celebrated series, "Details of Love." The product of romantic turmoil in his life, the images were created by the chemical bonding of color printing paper with the acidic entrails of slaughtered rabbits. The photogram in Fuss's hands expresses the direct, tactile, "gut-wrenching" conversion of the body's pain into an image swirling with emotion.

Indifferent to the "normal" pictures that can be found in news magazines, he has constantly changed course and revamped his technique. The traces left by nature in Fuss's work, the way the photograph reflects—is embedded with—the materials of its own making, are revealed only by the mysteries of light, which he has pushed to new extremes. In his "Black Children" series from 1990 he produced images so dark that they hover on the threshold of visibility. In his latest photograms, he has printed sections of shattered stained-glass windows and left the silver in the paper, an effect he likens to visiting a church by moonlight.

Like many of the early photographers, Fuss is as much inventor as artist. At the same time that he conceives of a new kind of picture he wants to make, he must also devise the tool that will allow him to carry out his idea. He has built multilevel, octopus-armed rigs to make enormous photograms of splashing water. His light sources have included handheld flashlights, powerful strobes, his enlarger, and the sun. He tends to elaborate his ideas through a series of pictures over a year or more rather than move in many directions at once.

Featured regularly in one-person shows through galleries, he has also appeared in numerous group shows at museums, including the "Whitney Biennial" in 1991. His work can be found in the permanent collections of the Metropolitan Museum, Whitney Museum, and Museum of Modern Art, in New York City, Los Angeles County Museum, Victoria and Albert Museum, in London, Australian National Gallery, and many other institutions.

He lives in New York City with his black rabbit, Rabbi Jacob.

**—Richard B. Woodward**

## Technical information

The photographs in this book were shot with a handmade pinhole camera onto which Fuss grafted an 8x10 film back. He used Tri-X and Plus-X film, depending on lighting conditions, and printed his negatives on Ilford Gallery Matte paper.